A Wedding Service Guide

A Resource for Officiants and Couples

Alan R. Kemp

Hermitage Desktop Press
P.O. Box 167
Vaughn, WA 98394

A Wedding Service Guide

A Resource for Officiants and Couples

Alan R. Kemp

Hermitage Desktop Press
P.O. Box 167
Vaughn, WA 98394

ISBN: 978-0692215470

Printed in the United States of America

TABLE OF CONTENTS

CHAPTER 1: USING THIS GUIDE

It is my sincere hope that this guide will help those who are planning a wedding to create a personalized ceremony that will be meaningful for everyone. It is intended as a resource for those who will be officiating and the couples themselves. It can be used by couples as a base on which to create their own individualized ceremony. Officiants can use the handbook to prepare custom ceremonies for those couples who want this service or as an aid to preparing ceremonies that can be put on the shelf so to speak.

FORMAT

This guide has been formated to make it easier to use. Example text can be chosen for the wedding, edited, modified, copied, and compiled as needed for your ceremony. Major topics or identification of the person who will be speaking will be placed in the left side margin, text to the right.

ORGANIZATION

The guide begins with an overview of common parts of the marriage ceremony. Reviewing this section is a good way for those not thoroughly familiar with the wedding service to gain a better understanding. Following this overview four samples for each part of the service are included: Civil, spiritualistic/non-denominational, contemporary, and traditional. Key parts of the traditional service, such as opening words, charge, vows, and ring exchange, are based upon the order of worship prescribed in the *Book of Common Prayer.* A good way to get ideas for writing your own service is to look at some examples and then modify them to suit your own personalities, values, and needs.

CHAPTER 2: OVERVIEW OF RESOURCES

Seven appendices are included as resources. They can be found in the back of the book.

CHECKLIST

Appendix 1: A wedding certemony checklist. Couples are encouraged to use the checklist as a way to identify those components of the wedding ceremony they want included in their ceremony, and to produce an "order of worship."

ORDER OF WORSHIP

Appendix 2: An "order of worship" form.

SCRIPTURE INDEX

Appendix 3: A sampling of Scripture references. Chapter and verse is indicated on the left, followed by a brief explanation of the general topic it relates to.

SECULAR PASSAGES

Appendix 4: Non-religious references appropriate for inclusion in ceremonies.

A FEW QUOTES

Appendix 5: A few brief quotes that may be appropriate for use in a homily, sermonette, or brief lecture.

ANNOTATED BIBLIOGRAPHY

Appendix 6: Annotated bibliography of wedding reference books, some of which may be available at local public libraries. Several of these references also include descriptions of such special variations as the Jewish wedding and the Moslem wedding. Of interest in the annotated bibliography are references to Catholic wedding books that specify specific options permitted in the Church. Those wishing a traditional mass or Catholic ceremony without a mass are referred to two such references.

REFERENCES

Appendix 7: Other references.

CHAPTER 3: SUGGESTED STEPS

You can use this book any way you like, however, you may find the following steps helpful.

1.   Pick it up and browse through it, paying no attention to order, familiarizing yourself with what's in it, spending time looking at what interests you.

2.   Read the overview of the parts of the wedding service.   Talk with your partner and discuss the parts you want in your ceremony.   Use the checklist as a way to provide you with an overview of what your ceremony might look like.

3.   Review the samples for each part you want and decide if you want to use one of the examples there as is, modify one, or write your own.   Use the appendixes to get you started with Scripture, readings, or quotations, but don't feel you have to limit yourselves to the ones there.

4.   Discuss with your officiant (the person who will officiate at the ceremony) what you want, and come to an agreement about what will be included in your ceremony.

5.   Decide on the "order of worship" or order in which the various parts of the ceremony will occur. If your pastor is affiliated with a specific denomination he may require that you follow the "order of worship" accepted by the denomination.

6.   You can use your "order of worship" as the framework from which you print a brief "program" that you can hand to guests as they arrive. If you have specific prayers or hymns that guests may not know, for example, this is a way to make sure "everyone is reading off the same sheet of music."

CHAPTER 4: THE BIG PICTURE

In this chapter, we take a big picture look at the wedding service, with all its elements. However, we should keep in mind that there is a great deal of variation in what one must include and what one may wish to include. n my state, Washington, the only element that is required for the solemnization of a marriage is that the two parties declare that they take each other to be the other's spouse. There is no particular prescribed text. Ceremonies can include as little as simple vows, be full traditional affairs, or be somewhere in between. It is up to the couple and the officiant to decide. Listed below are some common elements of a contemporary wedding ceremony, with a brief explanation of each.

ORDER OF WORSHIP

"Order of worship" is the term used to denote the components of the service and the sequence in which they will occur. This list of components of the wedding service is in a sequence that is consistent with a traditional order of worship. Even in traditional services the order of worship varies from denomination to denomination.

PROCESSION OR ENTRANCE

This refers to the entrance or procession of the wedding party.

OPENING WORDS

This is usually a welcome to those gathered and/or a call to worship.

INVOCATION

In traditional services this is a call to prayer, invocation of the trinity, or reminder that the wedding ceremony is a solemn event. This is often followed by an opening prayer. In a less formal sense it can be a way of helping those gathered achieve a deeper sense of spiritual consciousness or bonding with others and God.

READINGS/LITURGY OF THE WORD

In some traditional services the "Liturgy of the Word" occurs after the opening prayer. This is a reading of two or three Scripture passages, the last being from the Gospels. A Responsorial Psalm may sometimes be prayed or sung after the first reading and before a second reading. In the Catholic tradition the Gospel is always read by a priest or deacon. In less traditional services, readings from a variety of sources such as the poet Omar Khayyam, Shakespeare, or Kahlil Gibran may be substituted.

HOMILY, SERMON

In many ceremonies it is part of the order of worship to include a short homily or longer sermon. Homilies in liturgical, Catholic/Anglican, services tend to be short and sweet. In non-liturgical, Protestant, churches it is now more common to include a longer sermon or teaching.

If there is to be a full, traditional, service, perhaps including the celebration of Communion, the marriage portion of the ceremony, which following immediately below, will occur before communion (so the married couple can partake of this sacrament for the first time as a couple).

PRESENTING THE BRIDE

This is the part of the ceremony, where by tradition, the officiant asks, "Who give's this woman in marriage." It is now more often called "presenting the bride."

CHARGE TO COUPLE

It is during the "charge to the couple" portion of the ceremony when the officiant speaks to the couple directly, reminding them of the solemnity of marriage and the seriousness of the obligation they are about to undertake. In very traditional services, it is also the point at which either party, or anyone in attendance, with knowledge of reasons as to why the marriage may not legally proceed, is given the opportunity to state them.

CONSENT TO MARRY

The consent to marry is preparation for the actual vows. It is at this point when each party is asked to declare that they are entering into the marriage of their own free will.

VOWS

The vows speak for themselves. While the form of the vows may be specially written, it is the one part of the service that is legally necessary. This is the point at which each party declares or makes a vow to have the other as husband or wife.

RING EXCHANGE

It is common for bride and groom to exchange rings, a practice based upon Jewish tradition, in which the man offers something of value he owns to a prospective bride. When rings are exchanged it is sometimes appropriate for the officiant to bless the rings, or say a prayer over them, before they are exchanged. Not every couple chooses to exchange rings. For occupational safety reasons, not everyone wears them. Couples may also choose to exchange something other than a ring.

THE KISS

The couple are encouraged to seal their vows with a kiss. The officiant may indicate this with words, such as, "You may now kiss."

PRONOUNCING MARRIAGE

This is the point in the service when the person officiating the ceremony, after listening to the promises and vows, declares by the authority vested in him or her by the state, province, or religious denomination, that the couple is married.

BLESSING

After the marriage is pronounced, the officiant or couple often offer a prayer if it is a religious service. A benediction or blessing is often offered as a way to close the service.

LORDS PRAYER

The Lord's Prayer as identified in the New Testament (Matthew 6:9-13; Luke 11:2-4) is often included as part of the ceremony.

PASSING OF THE PEACE

Members of the gathered community may share a handshake, hug, or holy kiss as may be appropriate. The "passing of the peace" is a common part of religious worship in a number of churches. When it is included it precedes Communion, if Communion is celebrated. The officiant offers the exhortation, "Peace be with you." The couple share to those gathered and asks that they "pass the peace" to those around them in the same way. Since

COMMUNION

In Catholic, Anglican, and Orthodox liturgies, and some protestant services, communion is included in the service. For Christian couples, this is often because the bride and groom wish to share Christ's feast with friends and family. It is also often possible in these faith traditions to have a marriage ceremony outside of the celebration of the Eucharist, in which case communion does not occur.

FINAL BLESSING

At the conclusion of the ceremony, it may be appropriate for the officiant to offer a final blessing, if it is a religious service.

MUSIC

Music, either "live" in the form of a vocalist, other musician, or recorded selection can be used at various points.

CHAPTER 5: ORDER OF WORSHIP

"Order of worship" is the term used to denote the components of the service and the sequence in which they will occur. Even in traditional services the order of worship varies from denomination to denomination.

Following will be included two traditional orders of worship are based upon those in the current edition of *The Book of Common Prayer,* one with communion and one without. This is the accepted order of worship of the Episcopal Church and is similar to that of the Roman Catholic Church.

WITHOUT COMMUNION

1. Opening words
2. Ministry of the word

(One or more recommended Scriptures, including at least one of the Gospels)

3. The charge
4. Declaration of consent
5. Marriage vows
6. Blessing and exchange of rings
7. Pronouncement of marriage
8. Prayers.

(In Christian ceremonies may include Lord's Prayer. Please refer to current edition of *Book of Common Prayer)*

9. Blessing of the marriage

WITH COMMUNION

1. Opening words
2. Ministry of the word

One or more recommended Scriptures, including at least one of the Gospels.

3.   The charge
4.   Declaration of consent
5.   Marriage vows
6.   Blessing and exchange of rings
7.   Pronouncement of marriage
8.   Prayers

In Christian ceremonies, the prayers may include the Lord's Prayer, please refer to current edition of *Book of Common Prayer*

9.   Blessing of the marriage
10.   Passing the peace
11.   Communion or Eucharist
12.   Prayer

CHAPTER 6: SAMPLE RELIGIOUS CEREMONY

I commonly use the following when officiating at simple ceremonies which do not include communion.

Note: This ceremony can be used for opposite-sex marriages or adapted for same-sex marriages.

Note: Various other components, such as readings, music, etc., may be added to the basic service. See, for example, a variety of consents, vows, ring exchanges, readings, and so forth, contained in the Apprendices.

INTRODUCTORY WORDS

The officiant may wish to say a few informal word.

INVOCATION

Officiant: In the name of the Father, † Son, and the Holy Spirit. Amen.

ADDRESS TO THE PEOPLE

Officiant: Dearly beloved, we are gathered here together in the sight of God, and in the face of this congregation, to join together in the bonds of holy matrimony this man (or first party) and this woman (or second party), which is an honorable estate, not to be entered into lightly or wantonly, but reverently, discreetly, and soberly.

Into which estate these two persons come now to be joined. Therefore if anyone can show any just cause why they may not be lawfully joined, let them now speak or forever hold their peace.

PRESENTATION OF THE BRIDE

Officiant: Who presents this woman (or second party) to be married to this man (or first party)?

Presenter: I do.

CONSENT

Officiant: *(to the man, or first party)* Of your own free will, N., is it your it your intent to have N. to be your lawfully wedded wife (or husband)?
Man (or first party): It is.

Officiant: *(to the woman, or second party)* Of your own free will, N., is it your it your intent to have N to be your lawfully wedded husband (or wife)?
Woman (or second party): It is.

BLESSING BY THE CONGREGATION

I include a brief explanation about the nature of a blessing. Members of the congregation are advised that not only are we here to ask God's blessing but to extend ours as well. As part of their own blessing the congregation is asked if they promise to do all that they can to uphold and support this new marriage.

LITURGY OF THE WORD

If a reading is to be included in the marriage liturgy it is inserted here in the service.

LITURGY OF THE WORD

I include, here, the most possible verse from Scripture.

Officiant: The first reading is from the Apostle Paul on the Nature of Love.

1 Cor 13: 1-7, 13. "If I speak with the tongues of men and of angels, but do not have love, I have become a noisy gong or a clanging cymbal. If I have the gift of prophecy, and know all mysteries and all knowledge; and if I have all faith, so as to remove mountains, but do not have love, I am nothing.

And if I give all my possessions to feed the poor, and if I surrender my body to be burned, but do not have love, it profits me nothing.

Love is patient, love is kind and is not jealous; love does not brag and is not arrogant, does not act unbecomingly; it does not seek its own, is not provoked, does not take into account a wrong suffered, does not rejoice in unrighteousness, but rejoices with the truth; bears all things, believes all things, hopes all things, endures all things.

But now faith, hope, love, abide these three; but the greatest of these is love."

VOWS

This having been said, the woman (or second party) presents the man (or first party) with her right hand and the man (or first party) cradles it in his own

Officiant: Very well, then. (Turning to man, or first party) N., please repeat after me.

Officiant: I, N., take you, N., to be my wife (or husband), to have and to hold, from this day forward, for better, for worse, for richer, for poorer, in sickness and in health, to love, to cherish and to honor; and thereunto, in the presence of God, and with all that I am and all that I have. R. And so be it.

Officiant: (Turning to woman, or second party) N., please repeat after me.

Officiant: I, N., take you, N., to be my husband (or wife), to have and to hold, from this day forward, for better, for worse, for richer, for poorer, in sickness and in health, to love, to cherish and to honor; and thereunto, in the presence of God, and with all that I am and all that I have. R. And so be it.

The bridegroom and bride place the rings on a salver held before them by a server. The priest sprinkles the rings with holy water in the form of a cross and then blesses them saying:

Priest: Bless † O Lord and † hallow these rings, that they who wear them may ever keep true faith to the other, and so, abiding in your peace and in conformity with your holy will, may ever live together in unchanging love; through Christ our Lord. R. Amen.

The ring bearer is motioned to come closer

Officiant: N. (man, or first party), as you give N. (woman, or second party) your ring, please repeat after me.

Turning to man the priest asks him to take the woman's ring from the salver

Officiant: With this ring I thee wed; my truest love I thee pledge; with my body I give you reverence, and with all my strength I thee shield. R. Amen.

Man is then asked to place the ring on the woman's finger

Officiant: N. (woman, or second party) as you give N. (man, or first party) your ring, please repeat after me. *Turning to woman, or second party, the officiant asks her to take man's, or first party's, ring*

Officiant: With this ring I thee wed; my truest love I thee pledge; with my body I give you reverence, and with all my heart I thee unfold. R. Amen.

15

Woman, or second party, is then asked to place the ring on man's finger

The officiant joins the hands of the two parties. Here an anointing may take place

UNITY CANDLE - *OPTIONAL*

If the unity candle is to be lit it should be done here. While music is playing the bride and groom bring their lit candle to the large unity candle and then rejoin the officiant in the center of the sanctuary area.

ANOINTING

This is non-traditional. Brief explanation of anointing with oil as an ancient practice going back thousands of years, and an act designed to consecrate or set people or things aside for special purposes. Here we will consecrate the head, heart, and hands of each marriage partner.

Head - making the sign of the cross on each forehead

Officiant: With this holy oil we bless and consecrate your minds and your consciousness, that you might always remember the commitments you made today, that you grow in wisdom, and that you achieve a deep understanding of each other.

Heart - making the sign of the cross before each of the couple's hearts

Officiant: With this holy oil we bless and consecrate your hearts, that deep love and compassion for each other may grow and abide there, and that they are never dark or empty.

Hands - with palms up, and fingers touching, the priest draws a circle such that their hands are encompassed with the oil

Officiant: With this holy oil we bless and consecrate your hands, uniting the two of you. May it be that these hands are always used to hold and support each other; and to bring each other love and never hurt.

This concludes the anointing

DECLARATION & PRESENTATION

Officiant: Those whom God has joined together, let no one put asunder.

Officiant: Forasmuch as N. (man, or first party) and N. (woman, or second party) have consented together in holy wedlock and have witnessed the same before God and this company, and thereto have given and pledged their troth each to the other, and have declared the same by giving and receiving of a ring and joining hands: By the authority vested in me (by the Church, or the State, Province, County, etc., of...) I declare that they are married.

In the name of the Father, Son, and of the Holy Spirit.

      Or

May God the Father hold you in the palm of his hand †, the love of Christ be in your heart †, and may the Holy Spirit light your path †.

Officiant: You may now embrace and kiss one another
Officiant: Ladies and gentlemen, it my pleasure to present to you N. (man, or first party) and N. (woman, or second party), who are now married.

CHAPTER 7: SAMPLE NON-RELIGIOUS CEREMONY

I commonly use the following adaptation of a religious ceremony when officiating at non-religious ceremonies.

Note: This ceremony can be used for opposite-sex marriages or adapted for same-sex marriages.

Note: Various other components, such as readings, music, etc., may be added to the basic service. See, for example, a variety of consents, vows, ring exchanges, readings, and so forth, contained in the Apprendices.

INTRODUCTORY WORDS

The officiant may wish to say a few informal introductory words to the congregation.

ADDRESS TO THE PEOPLE

Officiant: Dearly beloved, we are gathered here together in the face of this congregation, to join together in the bonds of matrimony this man (or first party) and this woman (or second party), which is an honorable estate, not to be entered into lightly or wantonly, but reverently, discreetly, and soberly.

Into which estate these two persons come now to be joined. Therefore if anyone can show any just cause why they may not be lawfully joined, let them now speak or forever hold their peace.

PRESENTATION OF THE BRIDE

Officiant: Who presents this woman (or second party) to be married to this man (or first party)?

Presenter: I do.

CONSENT

Officiant: *(to the man, or first party)* Of your own free will, N., is it your it your intent to have N. to be your lawfully wedded wife (or husband)?
Man (or first party): It is.

Officiant: *(to the woman, or second party)* Of your own free will, N., is it your it your intent to have N to be your lawfully wedded husband (or wife)?
Woman (or second party): It is.

BLESSING BY THE CONGREGATION

I include a brief explanation about the nature of a blessing. Members of the congregation are advised that we are present to bless and witness this union. As part of this blessing the congregation is asked if they promise to do all that they can to uphold and support this new marriage.

READINGS

If one or more readings are to be included in the marriage ceremony it is inserted here in the service.

VOWS

This having been said, the woman (or second party) presents the man (or first party) with her right hand and the man (or first party) cradles it in his own

Officiant: Very well, then. (Turning to man, or first party) N., please repeat after me.

Officiant: I, N., take you, N., to be my wife (or husband), to have and to hold, from this day forward, for better, for worse, for richer, for poorer, in sickness and in health, to love, to cherish and to honor; and with all that I am and all that I have. R. And so be it.

Officiant: (Turning to woman, or second party) N., please repeat after me.

Officiant: I, N., take you, N., to be my husband (or wife), to have and to hold, from this day forward, for better, for worse, for richer, for poorer, in sickness and in health, to love, to cherish and to honor; and with all that I am and all that I have. R. And so be it.

RING EXCHANGE

The ring bearer is motioned to come closer

Officiant: N. (man, or first party), as you give N. (woman, or second party) your ring, please repeat after me.

Turning to man the priest asks him to take the woman's ring

Officiant: With this ring I thee wed; my truest love I thee pledge; with my body I give you reverence, and with all my strength I thee shield. R. Amen.

Man is then asked to place the ring on the woman's finger

Officiant: N. (woman, or second party) as you give N. (man, or first party) your ring, please repeat after me.

Turning to woman, or second party, the officiant asks her to take man's, or first party's, ring

Officiant: With this ring I thee wed; my truest love I thee pledge; with my body I give you reverence, and with all my heart I thee unfold. R. Amen.

Woman, or second party, is then asked to place the ring on man's finger

The officiant joins the hands of the two parties. Here an anointing may take place

UNITY CANDLE - *OPTIONAL*

If the unity candle is to be lit it should be done here. While music is playing the bride and groom bring their lit candle to the large unity candle and then rejoin the officiant in the center of the sanctuary area.

ANOINTING

This is non-traditional. Brief explanation of anointing with oil as an ancient practice going back thousands of years, and an act designed to consecrate or set people or things aside for special purposes. Here we will consecrate the head, heart, and hands of each marriage partner.

Head - making the sign of the cross on each forehead

Officiant: With this holy oil we bless and consecrate your minds and your consciousness, that you might always remember the commitments you made today, that you grow in wisdom, and that you achieve a deep understanding of each other.

Heart - making the sign of the cross before each of the couple's hearts

Officiant: With this holy oil we bless and consecrate your hearts, that deep love and compassion for each other may grow and abide there, and that they are never dark or empty.

Hands - with palms up, and fingers touching, the priest draws a circle such that their hands are encompassed with the oil

Officiant: With this holy oil we bless and consecrate your hands, uniting the two of you. May it be that these hands are always used to hold and support each other; and to bring each other love and never hurt.

21

This concludes the anointing

DECLARATION & PRESENTATION

Officiant: Those whom God has joined together, let no one put asunder.

Officiant: Forasmuch as N. (man, or first party) and N. (woman, or second party) have consented together in wedlock and have witnessed the same before this company, and have given and pledged their troth each to the other, and have declared the same by giving and receiving of a ring and by the joining of hands: By the authority vested in me I hereby declare they are married.

Officiant: You may now embrace and kiss one another

Officiant: Ladies and gentlemen, it my pleasure to present to you N. (man, or first party) and N. (woman, or second party), who are now married.

CHAPTER 8: OPENING WORDS

This is usually a welcome to those gathered and/or a call to worship. It is the act which begins the wedding ceremony, usually by the person who is officiating the ceremony.

Several options for "opening words" are included here. To facilitate putting together a complete ceremony each is listed on a separate page. Other parts of the ceremony, such as vows and token exchange, will follow the same format.

OPENING WORDS, OPTION 1 - CIVIL

Officiant: We are gathered here today to share with *(first party's first name)* and *(second party's first name)* and with each other as they join together in marriage.

The joining of lovers in matrimony is an honored and respected tradition throughout the world.

OPENING WORDS, OPTION 2 - NON-DENOMINATIONAL

Officiant: On behalf of *(man's, or first party's first name)* and I would like to welcome you. This gathering of family and friends represents much more than a collection of individuals, couples, or families. We are here to share in the experience of seeing a profound change in two lives. This alone creates a bond between us and with *(man's, or first party's first name)* and *(woman's, or second party's first name).* By you being here you bless this wedding and add to its significance.

OPENING WORDS, OPTION 3 - CONTEMPORARY

Officiant: We are gathered here today, in the presence of God and these witnesses, to join *(man's, or first party's first name)* and *(second party's first name)* in holy matrimony. *(First party's first name)* and *(second party's first name)* express their gratitude that you are here. Each of you has a special place in their hearts. You have cared for them, encouraged, and guided them at critical times.

OPENING WORDS, OPTION 4 - TRADITIONAL

Officiant: Dearly beloved: We are gathered here today, in the presence of God and in the face of this congregation to join together in the bonds of holy matrimony this man *(or woman)* and this woman *(or man)* in Holy Matrimony. The covenant of marriage was established by God, and our Lord, Jesus Christ, blessed this manner of life by his presence with the first miracle at a wedding in Cana. It signifies to us the mystery of the union between Christ and his Church, and Holy Scripture commends it to be honored among all people.

The union of husband and wife in heart, body, and mind is intended by God for their mutual joy; for the help and comfort given one another in prosperity and adversity; and, when it is God's will, for the procreation of children and their nurture in the knowledge and love of the Lord.

OPENING WORDS, OPTION 5 - WRITE YOUR OWN

CHAPTER 9: OPENING PRAYER

OVERVIEW

In traditional services this is a call to prayer and reminder that the wedding ceremony is a solemn event. In a less formal sense it can be a way of helping those gathered achieve a deeper sense of spiritual consciousness or bonding with the others gathered.

For civil ceremony

The invocation/opening prayer is most likely omitted from the civil ceremony, but vastly secularized version of an invocation has been included among the available options for a service.

Smudging option. Toward the end of the book in the "benediction" section we have included a "smudging option." This is a Native American blessing. If you wish to consider including a smudging you may also wish to introduce it at the beginning of the ceremony. You may wish to take the smudge bowl, or shell, to a place near the exit when the wedding concludes so that guests may partake of the smudge before they reenter the world.

OPENING PRAYER OPTION 1 - CIVIL

Officiant: Please join with me in a few moments of silence as we contemplate the significance of this event, and as we send our good thoughts and best wishes for the happiness and well being of *(man's, or first party's first name)* and *(woman's, or second party's first name)*.

Officiant: I ask each of you here to reflect a moment on what is to occur here today, and then ponder that as significant as this event might seem to us it is but a wisp in a greater wind that encompasses all of our spirits and all of our lives. In our hearts, let us seek greater understanding and truth about life, and let us join our spirits with *(first name of man, or first party)* and *(first name of woman, or second party)*. Let us add our wishes and prayers that the winds of life might blow favorably on their life together. Let us also add our wishes that they are able to find the strength and wisdom necessary to keep the vows they make here today. Move them to accomplish good things for themselves, their fellow human beings, their world; and that they add their song to the joy of life itself.

OPENING PRAYER, OPTION 3 - CONTEMPORARY

Officiant   Please join me in prayer. Dear God, we thank you for this day, for *(man's, or first party's, first name)* and *(woman's, or second party's, first name)*, and for their friends and families, who have loved and cared for them. *(rirst party's first name)* and *(second party's first name)* have chosen each other to be their lifelong companions and mates. They come here before this gathering to declare their love and ask that they be joined in matrimony. We ask that you grant them the faith, hope, and love to keep the vows they make here today, and that you bless them and sanctify this union. Amen.

OPENING PRAYER, OPTION 4 - TRADITIONAL

Officiant: Let us pray. Dear Lord, You have created us male and female in Your image, and have decreed that it is not good for man to be alone. *(Man's first name)* and *(woman's first name)* have come here today asking that they be united in marriage and seek your blessing. In the name of your Son, Jesus Christ, we ask that you bless and grace this marriage. We pray that with fidelity and love *(Man's first name)* and *(woman's first name)* will honor and keep the vows they make here today. In the name of the Father, the Son, and the Holy Spirit. Amen.

OPENING PRAYER OPTION 5 - WRITE/CHOOSE YOUR OWN

CHAPTER 10: READINGS/LITURGY OF THE WORD

In many wedding ceremonies today it has become more and more common for Scripture or literature readings to be included.

Scripture readings have long been a part of Anglican weddings and Roman Catholic weddings. Approved verses, and the approved order of worship itself are contained in the English translation of the *Rite of Marriage,* and in Episcopal services by the *Book of Common Prayer.*

Other Protestant weddings have tended to be less formal, but often do include one or more Scripture readings.

In some less religiously oriented weddings it is becoming more common for readings from literary works that seem appropriate to be read. This should be a choice made by the couple and officiant.

The appendixes include a number of Old Testament references, New Testament references, and literary titles to choose from. These are but a few of those that might be used. A number of quotes are also contained in the appendices.

In the pages that follow several commonly used passages will be reprinted.

READINGS/LITURGY, OPTION 1 - GEORGE ELLIOT

Because the writings of the great author's are often copyrighted materials, I can not include the quotes directly. Instead, I would like to encourage the reader to make an online search for George Elliot's words on love. Do the same for the authors named in the following sections.

READINGS/LITURGY, OPTION 2 - KAHLIL GIBRAN ON LOVE

READINGS/LITURGY, OPTION 3 - KAHLIL GIBRAN ON MARRIAGE

]READINGS/LITURGY, OPTION 4 - ST. PAUL ON LOVE

Please refer to any standard bible for the following Scripture quotation: *1 Cor 13: 3-5; 13*

READINGS/LITURGY, OPTION 5 - CHOOSE YOUR OWN

Please confer with the suggested readings in Annendix

CHAPTER 11: HOMILY, SERMON, OR LESSON

In Catholic and Episcopal ceremonies it is often part of the order of worship to include a homily (sermon). Today in many other protestant churches it is becoming more and more accepted to include a short sermon or teaching as part of the service itself.

Because homilies can vary greatly between officiant and officiant, I have not included specific samples. What I have done is included blank page on which a homily, lesson, or sermon can be outlined.

Scripture lessons can be based on any number of Scriptures, including any that were included in the Readings/Liturgy section of the ceremony. A number of additional Scriptures are included in the appendixes that you may wish to review.

If you do not wish the lesson to be based on a specific passage, or on the bible, you may wish to select a theme, an event in your life, or an issue that is important to you, and ask your officiant to develop a short lesson based on this theme.

HOMILY, LESSON, SERMON, THEME

Traditionally, the officiant would craft a homily, short serman, or lesson. However, it may be perfectly appropriate for someone among the couples family or friends to deliver a talk. One could choose any number of themes: the nature of the couples relationship and what this next step might mean to them; the nature of love; the nature of commitment; what it means to grow old together; how two people can complement and help each other; and, any number of others.

CHAPTER 12: CHARGE TO THE COUPLE

It is during "the charge" portion of the ceremony when the officiant speaks to the couple to remind them of the solemnity of marriage and the seriousness of the obligation they are about to undertake. It is also the point at which either party, or anyone in attendance, with knowledge of reasons as to why the marriage may not legally proceed, is traditionally given the opportunity to state them.

CHARGE TO THE COUPLE, OPTION 1 - CIVIL

Officiant: While marriage is an honored institution, it also carries grave personal and legal responsibilities. The laws of this state/province establish specific requirements for any who desire to become married, including that they are not already married, are of a required age, and obtain a license. Once you become married you will have legal and personal responsibilities for each other.

Do either of you know of any reasons why you may not be legally married?

(Wait for an appropriate amount of time to allow for a response)

If any of the witnesses are aware of any reason why this man and woman may not be lawfully joined in marriage, please state those reasons now.

(Barring any lawful objections, proceed)

Officiant: When two people join in the commitment of matrimony they become more than the sum of two lives. The relationship itself has a life. It is a profound experience and one that will irrevocably change your lives. It will also change your relationships with everyone else in your lives. For these reasons alone, if for no other, what we do here today carries grave responsibilities.

The way you deal with others, including the promises you make, has a profound impact on your character and your life. Marriage is a serious covenant and should not be entered into lightly, but only if you have truly thought through what you are doing and you are sure it is right.

The seriousness of this decision should not, however, overshadow your faith. Faith in each other and belief in what can be.

I not only charge you to seriously consider what you do here today, but to have the courage to truly live life. Strive to understand yourself and others as human beings. Be willing to ask important questions and endeavor for awareness and understanding in all things.

Seek that which is right and do it.

CHARGE TO THE COUPLE, OPTION 3 - CONTEMPORARY

Officiant   *(Man's, or first party's, first name)* and *(woman's, or second party's, first name)* have talked about what married life means to them, both the joys and challenges. They have considered the seriousness of this step, including difficulties they cannot even foresee. They know that at times these difficulties may test their ability to learn patience and acceptance. Understanding all this they have decided, nevertheless, that they wish to make this lifelong commitment to each other. They are making this choice because they also understand that the rewards of lifelong love are worth it. They are blessed with faith in their love and each other.

CHARGE TO THE COUPLE, OPTION 4 - TRADITIONAL

Officiant: Marriage is not to be entered into unadvisedly or lightly, but reverently, deliberately, and in accordance with the purposes for which it was instituted by God.

To those gathered Into this holy estate *(man's, or first party's, first name)* and *(woman's first name)* come now to be joined. If anyone here can show why they may not be lawfully be joined together, let him speak now or forever hold his peace.

To bride/groom, I require and charge you both, here in the presence of God, that if either of you knows why you may not be lawfully united in marriage, and in accordance with God's Word, you do now confess it.

CHARGE TO THE COUPLE, OPTION 5 - WRITE YOUR OWN

33

CHAPTER 13: DECLARATION OF CONSENT

The consent to marry is preparation for the actual vows themselves. It is at this point when each party is asked to declare that they are making a willing choice to enter into the marriage. Sometimes the consent is combined with the actual vows, and becomes almost part of the vows. In the Catholic Church the consent constitutes the vow itself, after which the priest declares, "What God has joined, let no man put asunder!"

DECLARATION OF CONSENT, OPTION 1 - CIVIL

Officiant   *(Man's, or first party's, first name)* and *(woman's, or second party's, first name)* you are here before me and these witnesses for the purpose of becoming joined in matrimony. We have already discussed the seriousness of this step. I ask now if you are taking this step of your own free will and without coercion.

The two parties: I am.

Officiant: If then it is your will to be married I will soon ask you to make your vows.

DECLARATION OF CONSENT, OPTION 2 - SPIRITUAL

Officiant to the two parties *(Man's, or first party's first name)* and *(woman's, or second party's, first name)*, are you seeking to be married of your own free will, realizing the profound changes that will occur in your life; promising to cherish, respect, and commit to your betrothed as your partner for the remainder of your life; remain faithful during hard times, and share in times of triumph; seek ever growing understanding and meaning in life, and respect your partner's right to do the same.

The two parties: I am.

Officiant to first party *(first name)*, Will you have *(second party's first name)* to be your wife, to share your life with her, in the state of holy matrimony? Will you love her (him), comfort her (him), honor and be loyal to her (him) in sickness and in health; and promise to be faithful to her alone, so long as you both live?

First party: I will.

Officiant to second party *(first name)*, will you have *(first party's first name)* to be your husband (wife), to share your life with him, in the state of holy matrimony? Will you love him (her), comfort him (her), honor and be loyal to him (her) in sickness and in health; and promise to be faithful to him (her) alone, so long as you both live?

Second party: I will.

Officiant to first party *(first name)*, will you have this woman to be your wedded wife, to live together after God's ordinance in the holy state of matrimony? Will you love her, comfort her, honor and keep her in sickness and in health; and forsaking all others, be faithful only unto her, so long as you both shall live?

First Party: I will.

Officiant to second party *(first name)*, will you have this man to be your wedded husband, to live together after God's ordinance in the holy state of matrimony? Will you love him, comfort him, honor and keep him in sickness and in health; and forsaking all others, be faithful only unto him, so long as you both shall live?

Second Party: I will.

DECLARATION OF CONSENT, OPTION 5 - CHOOSE YOUR OWN

CHAPTER 14: GIVING/PRESENTING THE BRIDE

"Giving" the bride has been a tradition in western marriages. *The Book of Common Prayer* included it as a standard part of the wedding solemnization ceremony until its 1979 revision. In western European culture women and children were regarded as chattel or property. Sensitivity about the status of women has increased more recently, and now "giving" the bride during the wedding still occurs but less commonly. The 1979 version of *The Book of Common Prayer* allows for the use of the word "presents" instead of "gives."

Many couples like to include a presentation of the bride as part of the ceremony. It may follow the traditional format where the minister says, "Who gives (presents) this woman to be married to this man."

It is also now quite acceptable for children of the bride, close friends, or other family members. In traditional marriages it is also an option within the *The Book of Common Prayer* for the parents of both bride and groom to present their respective son and daughter.

When "presentation" occurs it usually occurs after the exchange of "consents" and before the exchange of the actual vows.

CHAPTER 15: VOWS

The vows speak for themselves. While the form of the vows may be specially written, it is the one part of the service that is required. This is where each party declares or makes a vow to take the other in matrimony.

In my state, for instance, it is the only part of the wedding ceremony that is required under the law.

Vows sometimes get confused with "consents" that include wording to the effect: "Will you...." In Catholic wedding the "I wills" are the vows. The traditional protestant ceremony has both, though there is no reason, unless it is a requirement of your church's order of worship, why this has to be so.

VOWS, OPTION 1 - CIVIL

Officiant: *(to the first party)* Do you *(party's first name)* take this woman (man) to be your lawful wife (husband); to love her (him), comfort her (him), and respect her (him); in good times and bad; accepting her (him) for who she (he) is, with her (his) strengths and failings; forsaking all others; and, promise to be faithful to her (him)?

First party: I do.

Officiant" *(to the second party)* Do you *(party's first name)* take this man (woman) to be your lawful husband (wife); to love him (her), comfort him (her), and respect him (her); in good times and bad; accepting him (her) for who he (she) is, with strengths and failings; forsaking all others; and, promise to be faithful only to him (her)?

Second party: I do.

VOWS, OPTION 2 - NON-DENOMINATIONAL

Officiant: When two human beings make a solemn vow to each other a special relationship develops that involves not only their futures but their very spirit and being.

Officiant: *(first party's first name),* I will now ask you to make your solemn vows to *(second party's first name).* Please repeat after me.

First party: "I *(first name)* pledge myself to be your husband (or wife); to love you, care for you, encourage, and support you; to be a help to you and respect you. I promise to be faithful to you. I pledge myself to be your life partner; be there when times are hard, learning what I can, and to be there when times are good to celebrate life's joys with you.

Officiant: *(second party's first name),* I will now ask you to make your solemn vows to *(first party's name).* Please repeat after me,

Second party: "I *(first name)* pledge myself to be your husband (or wife); to love you, care for you, encourage, and support you; to be a help to you and respect you. I promise to be faithful to you. I pledge myself to be your life partner; be there when times are hard, learning what I can, and to be there when times are good to celebrate life's joys with you.

VOWS, OPTION 3 - CONTEMPORARY

Officiant: Officiant to first party *(first name),* since it is your will to proceed, please join your right hands.

Officiant to first party: Please repeat after me: I *(first name)* choose you *(first name),* to be my wife; to love and embrace, to be my partner and companion, to support and encourage, in good times and bad, as long as we both shall live.

Officiant to second party: Please repeat after me: I *(first name)* choose you *(first name),* to be my spouse; to love and embrace, to be my partner and companion, to support and encourage, in good times and bad, as long as we both shall live.

VOWS, OPTION 4 - TRADITIONAL

Officiant: (to bride and groom) *(first name of bride and groom),* since it is your will to proceed, please join your right hands.

Officiant: (to groom) Please repeat after me: I *(man's first name)* take you *(woman's first name),* to be my wife, to have and to hold from this day forward, for better for worse, for richer for poorer, in sickness and in health, to love and to cherish, until death us do part, according to God's holy ordinance; and thereto I plight thee my troth.

Officiant: (to bride) *(woman's first name),* since it is your will to proceed, please repeat after me: I *(woman's first name)* take *(man's first name),* to be my wedded husband, to have and to hold, from this day forward, for better, for worse, for richer, for poorer, in sickness and in health, to love and to cherish, till death us do part, according to God's holy ordinance; and thereto I plight thee my troth.

VOWS, OPTION 5 - CHOOSE YOUR OWN

CHAPTER 16: RING EXCHANGE

It is common for bride and groom to exchange rings, a practice based upon Jewish tradition in which the man offered something of value he owned to a prospective bride.

When rings are exchanged it is common for the officiant to bless the rings before they are exchanged. Not every couple chooses to exchange rings, and may choose not to exchange tokens at all. Sometimes couples choose to exchange something other than a ring, such as a rose. One party may want a ring whereas the other, for any number of reasons, may opt not to have one.

The following ring/token exchange examples are based on the assumption that rings are being exchanged. If they are not to be included as part of the ceremony, modification of the text will need to be done.

RING/TOKEN EXCHANGE, OPTION 1 - CIVIL

Officiant: *(to first party) (first name)* I would now like to ask you to give your ring (to *(first name)* and repeat after me: "I *(first name)* give you this ring (or token) as a symbol and reminder of the vows I made to you today and as an expression of my love.

Officiant: *(to second party) (first name)* I would now like to ask you to give your ring (or token) to *(first name)* and repeat after me: "I *(first name)* give you this ring as a symbol and reminder of the vows I made to you today and as an expression of my love.

RING/TOKEN EXCHANGE, OPTION 2 - SPIRITUAL

Officiant: If we look at these rings we can see that they are made of precious metal. Rings have no beginnings and no end. Rings can be thought of as circles that represent the ever evolving, ever turning, cycles of life itself. The ring is a reminder that we are part of something greater than ourselves. These rings are symbols of what occurs here today: the exchange of love, vows, and the merging of two lives, two human beings, two spirits, who will partake of life together as partners. May you always return to each other.

Officiant: *(to first party)* *(first name)* I would now like to ask you to give your ring (or your token) to *(woman's first name)* and repeat after me: "I *(first name)* give you this ring as a symbol of the promises I have made to you today, the life we share with all other things, and the life we will share as we pass through life's stages together.

Officiant: (to second party) *(first name)* I would now like to ask you to give your ring to *(first name)* and repeat after me: "I *(first name)* give you this ring as a symbol of the promises I have made to you today, the life we share with all other things, and the life we will share together as we pass through life's stages together.

RING EXCHANGE, OPTION 3 - CONTEMPORARY

Officiant: (taking the rings) Bless, O Lord, these rings, which have no beginning and no end, as a token of their love, and symbol of their vows and of life everlasting. Bless they who will wear them that they may abide in peace throughout the days of their lives.

Officiant: *(to first party)* *(handing the second party's ring to the first party)* Please place this ring on the third finger of *(woman's first name)* left hand, and repeat after me: "Take this ring as a token of my love and symbol of my vows and life everlasting."

42

Officiant: *(to second party) (handing the ring to the bride)* Please place this ring on the third finger of *(first party's first name)* left hand, and repeat after me: ""Take this ring as a token of my love and symbol of my vows and life everlasting."

Officiant: Bless O Lord, these rings to be a sign of the vows by which this man and this woman have bound themselves to each other; through Jesus Christ our Lord. Amen.

Groom: *(woman's first name)* I give you this ring as a symbol of my vow, and with all that I am, and all that I have, I honor you, in the Name of the Father, the Son, and the Holy Spirit (or in the Name of God).

Bride: *(man's first name)* I give you this ring as a symbol of my vow, and with all that I am, and all that I have, I honor you, in the Name of the Father, the Son, and the Holy Spirit (or in the Name of God).

RING EXCHANGE, OPTION 5 - WRITE YOUR OWN

CHAPTER 17: PRONOUNCING MARRIAGE

This is the point in the service when the person officiating the ceremony, after listening to the promises and vows, declares by the authority vested in him or her that the couple is married.

In religious ceremonies that include communion it is traditional to dispense the Eucharist after pronouncing marriage and before the ceremony or mass concludes.

PRONOUNCING MARRIAGE, OPTION 1 - CIVIL

Officiant: *(first party's first name)* and *(second party's first name)*, you have expressed your desire to be married and have been issued a marriage license. You have made solemn vows to each other and exchanged tokens of your promises in the presence of me and these witnesses. Therefor, by the authority granted me by *(name of state or province)* I now declare that you are *(choose a title for the role of each)*. You may now kiss.

PRONOUNCING MARRIAGE, OPTION 2 - NON-DENOMINATIONAL

Officiant: By exchanging solemn vows and tokens in the presence of me and those here gathered *(first name)* and *(first name)* have become more than just two individuals. You remain two unique and autonomous human beings but are now also partners in marriage, a relationship that affords new opportunities for love. By the authority invested in me I now declare what has already become a reality: that you are husband and wife. You may now kiss.

Officiant: Since *(first name)* and *(first name)* have consented to be married, have given their solemn vows before God and these witnesses, have pledged their love to each other, and have declared the same by exchanging a symbol of their love; I now pronounce that they are husband and wife (or married). Amen.

PRONOUNCING MARRIAGE, OPTION 4 - TRADITIONAL

Officiant   Now that *(first name)* and *(first name)* have given themselves to each other by solemn vows, with the joining of hands, and by the giving and receiving of a ring, I hereby pronounce that they are husband and wife, in the Name of the Father, and of the Son, and of the Holy Spirit.

What God has joined together let no one put asunder.

Those gathered: Amen.

PRONOUNCING MARRIAGE, OPTION 5 - CHOOSE YOUR OWN

CHAPTER 18: THE LORD'S PRAYER

The Lord's Prayer as identified in the New Testament (Matthew 6:9-13; Luke 11:2-4) is often included as part of the ceremony. It is part of the Catholic mass and is also frequently used in protestant services. One reason for its use is that prayer often follows solemn events such as marriage vows and that scripture says that this is the way Christ taught his followers how to pray.

There are at least two versions of the prayer that vary according to the use of the words "trespass" or "sin." The prayer will also vary slightly depending upon the version of the Bible being used.

CHAPTER 19: HOLY COMMUNION

In Catholic masses and some protestant services, communion is included as part of the service. It is also possible within the Roman Catholic Church to have a marriage ceremony, which is not part of a nuptial mass, in which case communion does not occur. When communion is part of the mass, it occurs after the marriage rite, which may be thought of as an extension of the homily, and which becomes the first official act as husband and wife. The sacrament of communion will vary from denomination to denomination.

Because communion is such a sacred part of faith, you should consult closely with the minister of your denomination if you wish to include or exclude communion as part of your wedding ceremony.

CHAPTER 20: FINAL BLESSING

After the marriage is pronounced in traditional weddings, the officiant will commonly lead the congregation in prayer. *The Book of Common Prayer* begins this with a recitation of the Lord's Prayer. The blessing or benediction will follow this.

In less formal weddings the prayer may be omitted but a benediction offered. In civil ceremonies, while not religious in nature, it is still common to offer a benediction of some kind. The benediction examples that follow do not necessarily assume that formal prayer has preceded it.

FINAL BLESSING, OPTION 1 - BENEDICTION OF THE APACHE

In order to protect copyright, the benediction of the Apache is not reprinted here. Instead the user is encouraged to conduct a search on the web, where it is readily available.

FINAL BLESSING, OPTION 2 - SMUDGING

Officiant: Native American elders tell us that all ceremonies must be entered into with a good heart so that we can pray, sing, and walk in a sacred manner and enter the sacred realm.

(rattle or drum) Native people throughout the world use herbs to accomplish this. A Native American ceremony that is becoming more popular today is to burn sage and sweetgrass, and along with prayer, to use it to purify and to bless. Those who are partaking in the blessing take the smoke into their hand and spread it on their faces, chest, and in their hair. This is called "smudging." *(first party's first name)* and *(second party's first name)* have asked that we bless their wedding with a smudging

ceremony. At the end of the ceremony we will place a smudge pot with sage and sweetgrass near the exit and I invite any of you who would like to partake in the blessing to partake of the smoke, and rub it onto your face, hands, and body.

Officiant and assistant: *(Light sage and sweetgrass bundles, or bits of wood in a smudge bowl to sprinkle sage, sweetgrass and cedar bits on.)*

BENEDICTION

(rattle or drum) In the name of all that is good, we ask a blessing for this man and woman who are married this day. We ask that the vows that they take here today are made sacred. We also ask that their hearts be purified so that they may enter into married life with a good spirit. We ask that they share many days and nights with love in their hearts. We ask that all of us here are able to help each other in this life and to become better human beings. We ask that all those who are gathered here share in this blessing and take it back into the world so that it might spread there, too. All these things we ask in the name of all that is good. We will now place the smudge pot near the exit so that all who wish may partake.

Assistant or guest (Places the smudge pot on a stand near the exit)

BENEDICTION OR BLESSING, OPTION 3 - CONTEMPORARY

Officiant: God the Father, Son, and Holy Spirit, bless, preserve, and keep you; the Lord mercifully look upon you with favor, and fill you with His Grace; that you may live this life in joy, and that you may have life everlasting. Amen.

Officiant: Most gracious God, we give you thanks for your tender love in sending Jesus Christ to come among us, to be born of a human mother, and to make the way of the cross to be the way of life. We thank you, also, for consecrating the union of man and woman in his Name. By the power of your Holy Spirit, we ask that You pour out the abundance of your blessing upon this man and this woman. Defend them against every enemy. Lead them into all peace. Let their love for each other be a seal upon their hearts, a mantle about their shoulders, and a crown upon their foreheads. Bless them in their work and in their companionship; in their sleeping and in their waking; in their joys and in their sorrows; in their life and in their death. Finally, in your mercy, bring them to that table where your saints feast for ever in your heavenly home; through Jesus Christ our Lord, who with you and the Holy Spirit lives and reigns, one God, for ever and ever. Amen.

Or this prayer, O God, you have so consecrated the covenant of marriage that in it is represented the spiritual unity between Christ and his Church: Send therefore your blessing upon these your servants, that they may so love, honor, and cherish each other in faithfulness and patience, in wisdom and true godliness, that their home may be a haven of blessing and peace; through Jesus Christ our Lord, who lives and reigns with you and the Holy Spirit, on God, now and for ever. Amen.

(Man/woman kneeling) God the Father, God the Son, God the Holy Spirit, bless, preserve, and keep you; the Lord mercifully with his favor look upon you, and fill you with all spiritual benediction and grace; that you may faithfully live together in this life, and in the age to come have life everlasting. Amen.

PASSING OF THE PEACE

The "passing of the peace" is a common part of Christian religious Eucharistic worship in a number of churches. The officiant offers the exhortation, "Peace be with you," to those gathered and asks that they pass the "peace be with you" to those around you to those others around them in the same way. In Catholic weddings it often follows the nuptial blessing and before celebration of Communion or the Eucharist. In some other churches it is done at the conclusion of the service.

RECESSIONAL OR EXIT

It is customary for the bride and groom to lead the wedding party, by twos, to the front door of the church, followed by maid of honor and best man, and then remainder of the wedding party.

A church is not always used for weddings, and there are many variations of the recessional that can be built into a ceremony.

APPENDIX A - WEDDING CEREMONY WORKSHEET

Procession or Entrance
Opening Words
Option:
Invocation/Opening Prayer
Option:
Readings/Liturgy:
Homily, Lesson, Sermon
Theme:
Giving the Bride
Option:
"The Charge"
Option:
Consent to Marry
Option:
Required: Vows
Option:
Ring/Token Exchange
Option:
Pronouncing Marriage
Option:
Holy Communion
Passing of the Peace
Method:
Benediction or Blessing
Option:
Recession or exit:
Music:

APPENDIX B - SELECTED BIBLE PASSAGES

HEBREW SCRIPTURES

Genesis 1:26-31 — God makes man & woman
Genesis 2:18-25 — Not good for man to be alone; God makes joins man and woman as one flesh
Genesis 24:48-51, 58-67 — Rebekah and Isaac
Ruth 1:16-17 — "Wherever you go, I will go"
Isaiah 61:10 62:5 — I will greatly rejoice in the Lord
Ps 19:4-5 — The sun is like a bridegroom
Ps 67 — God be merciful to us and bless us
Ps 127 — Prospering with the Lord
Prov 5:19 — Be intoxicated with your wife's love
Prov 7:18 — Let us take our fill of love till morning
Eccl 1:1-8 — What profit has a man...
Eccl 3:1-10; 8 — There is a time for love
Eccl 9:9 — Enjoy life with the wife you love
Song 1:4 — Your love is better than wine
Song 2:5; 5:8 — I am faint with love
Song 7:12 — I will give you my love
Song 8:6 — Love is as strong as death
Song 2:8-10, 14, 16 — The Shulamite
Song 3:1-6 — The Shulamite seeks her true love
Song 8:6-7 — The Shulamite to her beloved
Jeremiah 31:31-34 — New covenant with the house of Israel
Hosea 2:19-21 — I will betroth you in righteousness
Mal 2:14-15— Do not break faith with the wife of your youth

Matt 5:1-16 — The beatitudes
Matt 7:21, 24-29 — Things that count with God
Matt 19:3-6 — Christ's teaching on divorce
Matt 22:35-40 — What is the great commandment
Mark 10:6-9 — God made Man and Woman; Man will leave his parents and cleave to his wife
John 2:1-11 — First miracle at Cana
John 4:7-18 — Woman of Samaria
John 15:9-17 — Abide in Christ's love
John 17:21-24 — That they may be one in us
Romans 12:1-3, 9-18 — Be transformed by renewing your mind
1 Cor 7:3-5 — The husband and wife should fulfil their duty to each other
1 Cor 12:31-13:7 — Characteristics of love
1 Cor 8: — Love never fails
Eph 1:15, 28, 33 — Husbands, love your wives
Eph 3:14-21 — The Father grant you strength
Eph 5:28-33 — Man shall leave his parents and join his wife
Phil 4:4-9 — Be anxious for nothing; Meditate on virtues and good things
1 John 3:18-24 — Perfect love casts out fear
1 John 4:7-12 — Let us love one another
Col 3:12-17 — Importance of forgiveness and love
Heb 13:4 — Let marriage be held in honor and the marriage bed be undefiled
Pet 1:7 — Husbands be considerate of your wives
Rev 19:1, 5-9 — Blessed are they who are called to the marriage supper of the Lamb

APPENDIX C - NON-RELIGIOUS PASSAGES

William Shakespeare — Sonnet 116
Elizabeth Barrett Browning — Sonnet 43:"How Do I Love Thee?"
Kahlil Gibran — "Love gives not but itself..."
Kahlil Gibran — "Love One Another, but Make Not a Bond of Love"
James Russel Lowell — "True Love is but a Humble, Lowborn Thing"
John Ciardi — "Men Marry What they Need"
E. E. Cummings — "I carry our heart with me"
Gerald M. Hopkins — "At the Wedding March"
Carl Sandburg — "There is a Place Where Love Begins
Philip Sidney — "Love's Tranquility"
Stephen Sondheim — "Make of Our Hands, One Hand"
Matthew Arnold — "Dover Beach"

Richard Wagner — The Bridal Chorus (known as "Here comes the Bride")

Johannes S .Bach — Air on the G String

Johannes S. Bach — Arioso

Rachmaninoff (18th Vers.) — Rhapsody on a Theme of Paganini

G. F. Handel — The Water Music Series by Gramophone   Mad About.....

Nina Simone — My Baby Just Cares for Me

Johann Pachelbel — Canon

Felix Mendelssohns — Wedding March (from A Midsummer's Night Dream)

John Stanley or Clarke — Trumpet Voluntary

Arthur Bliss— Wedding Fanfare

Ludwig van Beethoven — Ode to Joy

Johannes S. Bach — Air on G String

Marc Antoine Charpentier — Prelude to "Te Deum"

G.F. Han — La Rejouissance from "Fireworks Music"

APPENDIX E - ANNOTATED BIBLIOGRAPHY

Aridas, C. (1969). *Your Catholic Wedding.* Garden City, N.Y.: Image Books.

A practical book about the Catholic wedding that includes explanation of the Church's view of the marriage rite, documents required by the Church, discussion of rules about interfaith marriages sanctified in the Church, discussion of Mass/Celebration options, options for each of the required or optional components of the service.

Brill, M., Halpin, M., and Genne, W. H. (1985). *Write Your Own Wedding.* Piscataway, N.J.: New Century Publishers, Inc.

Emphasizes three types of weddings: Roman Catholic, Jewish, and Protestant. Examples of complete services for each. Contains a collection of resources: Opening words, words of welcome, marriage credo, vows, rite of marriage, exchange of rings, prayers, readings, and emerging symbols. Also has a very complete section dealing with music for your wedding.

Glusker, D. & Misner, P. (1986). *Words for Your Wedding.* San Francisco: Harper & Rowe (Perennial Library).

A cleanly written book that includes options derived from a variety of churches for each of the orders of worship. Clean explanation of each of the orders of worship. Includes a section on special services: civil ceremony, Roman Catholic and ecumenical wedding, The Jewish wedding, writing your own service, and renewal of vows.

Homburg, A. (1985). *A New Wedding Service for You.* Lima, OH: C.S.S.. Publishing Co., Inc.

Contains nineteen orders of worship for the prospective bride and groom.

Klausner, A. (1986). *Weddings: A Complete Guide to All Religious and Interfaith Marriage Services.* Columbus, OH: Alpha Publishing Company.

A concise guide to the wedding, including a brief description of each part. Includes a checklist of things to be done at various time points before the wedding. Includes sample protestant wedding services including Episcopal, Presbyterian, Methodist, contemporary, and Unitarian. Also included are a Roman Catholic service, Jewish services, examples of interfaith weddings, Orthodox Christian, and Muslim.

Schwerin, J., Laketon, L., and Spence, A. (1985). *Wedding Styles.* New York: William Morrow and Co.

This is a two part book. The first part of the book is a series of beautifully executed photos on various types of services and the various parts of the wedding: rings, the cake, linens, gifts, the music, and the flowers. Part two of the book has a very clean system for tracking the guests, the wedding budget, people to send announcements to, booking all the professionals: clergy, organist, soloist, printer, florist, photographer, caterer, baker, musicians, and other.

Stein, M. & Graham, W.C. (1988). *The Catholic Wedding Book.* New York: Paulist Press.

Another practical book on the Catholic marriage, but with less emphasis on the options during the rite and more on other aspects of the marriage such as: the cast (includes a section on the duties of best man and maid of honor), selecting a church, selecting music, decorations for the church, etc. Also discussion of options during the Mass of ceremony, including readings. Sample program in back of book. Sample forms required by the Church.

Van Deusen, G.C.. (1987). *I Need to do What?! A Wedding Guide for the Groom, Best Man, and Ushers.* Cincinnati, OH: Tryke Books.

A concise book that concerns itself with the responsibilities of the best man, including: keeping the ring to be presented, distributing the envelopes with gratuities, coordinating ushers, arranging transportation, toasting, etc. Includes a best man's check list.

---- (1991). *Holy Bible, King James Version.* New York: Ivy Books.

---- (1982). *Holy Bible, New King James Version.* Nashville, TN: Thomas Nelson, Inc.

Day, A. C. (1992). *Roget's Thesaurus of the Bible.* New York: HarperCollins Publishers.

Episcopal Church. (1945).*The Book of Common Prayer.* Church Pension Fund.

Episcopal Church. (1979).*The Book of Common Prayer.* Church Hymnal Corporation & Seabury Press.

Fitzgerald, E. (Trans.) *Rubiaiyat of Omar Khayyam.* New York:Avenel Books.

Gibran, K. (1992). *The Phophet.* New York: Alfred A. Knopf, Inc.

Henry, L. C. (1945). *Five Thousand Quotes for all Occasions.* Garden City, NY: Doubleday & Co., Inc.

John-Roger, and McWilliams, P. (1991). *Life 101.* New York: Bantam Books.

Lamsa, G. M. (1957). *The Holy Bible from Ancient Eastern Manuscripts.* Philadelphia, PA: A. J. Holman & Co.

Lutheran Church in America et al. (1978). *Lutheran Book of Worship (Ministers Desk Edition).* Minneapolis, MN: Augsburg Publishing House.

Seldes, G. (1990). *The Great Quotations.* New York: Carol Publishing Group.

Shakespeare, W. (1961). *The Sonnets of William Shakespeare.* New York: Crown Publishers, Inc.

Storm, H. (1972). *Seven Arrows.* New York: Ballantine Books.

www.ingramcontent.com/pod-product-compliance
Lightning Source LLC
Chambersburg PA
CBHW031332040426
42443CB00005B/302